The Heart Swindler

How to Reclaim Your Heart and Stop Falling for
Liars, Losers, and Lunatics

Michelle Hill

© 2023 by Michelle Hill

No part of this publication may be reproduced, distributed, or transmitted in any form or by any means, including photocopying, recording, or other electronic or mechanical methods, or by any information storage and retrieval system without the prior written permission of the publisher, except in the case of very brief quotations embodied in critical reviews and certain other noncommercial uses permitted by copyright law.

This book is not intended for use as a source of legal, health, medical, or financial advice. All readers are advised to seek the services of competent professionals in these fields.

The advice and strategies found within may not be suitable for every situation. This work is sold with the understanding that neither the author nor the publisher is held responsible for the results accrued from the advice in this book.

For more information, visit https://HeartSwindler.com
For bulk book orders, contact Michelle Hill at michelle@heartswindler.com

ISBN-978-1-7346467-6-4 (paperback)
ISBN-978-1-7346467-7-1 (eBook)
Library of Congress Control Number: 2023916012

Publisher: Winning Champion Press, LLC, Smithfield, NC
Cover Design by Kelly Nielsen, Studio 92
https://www.studio92.us/
Book Interior and E-book Design by Amit Dey | amitdey2528@gmail.com

The stories and accounts in this book are based on true events, although names, places, and identifying characteristics have been changed to protect the identities of all involved.

DEDICATION

This book is dedicated to all the women who are survivors of liars, losers, and lunatics, yet have chosen to courageously continue their life's journey with boldness, brilliance, and beauty.

Special Bonus Gifts from Michelle

Being a survivor of a liar, loser, or lunatic from relationship deception leaves most women feeling betrayed, wounded, and left to deal with a lot of heartache.

I've personally experienced this heartbreak, and I know all too well how challenging it is to find support and resources to heal and work toward rebuilding your life and reclaiming your heart.

This is why I created TWO VALUABLE BONUS GIFTS to help you heal as you move forward on your journey toward wholeness.

Get your bonuses at:
https://heartswindler.com/Book-Bonuses

Bonus #1 – Resources to Inform and Heal

Michelle's thoughtfully curated collection of resources is designed to support, educate, and inspire you on your journey to healing and transformation.

Bonus #2 - Heartbeats to Healing: 8 Self-Care Ways to Heal from Relationship Deception

An inspiring guide to help you regain your confidence, self-worth, and inner contentment after experiencing relationship betrayal.

TABLE OF CONTENTS

Introduction ix

PART I – LIARS 1
   1. The Dutiful Girlfriend and Wife 3
   2. Gotta Watch Out for Those Online Dating Scams 13

PART II – LOSERS 19
   3. Future Fakers 21
   4. Newly Divorced. Newly Single. 35

PART III – LUNATICS 43
   5. The Long-Term Narcissistic Husband 45
   6. Narcissistic Abuse on Steroids 55

Conclusion 63
10 Red Flags You Absolutely, Positively MUST Watch Out For 67
About the Author 71
Connect with Michelle 77
Personal Reflection 79

INTRODUCTION

*I*t's August 18, 2004. As I drive the handsome, well-built man I met online four months ago to LAX for his flight home, my heart breaks in a million pieces. The immense feelings of betrayal, disillusionment, and shame engulf my entire body and soul. It's all I can do to hold back the tears, anger, and bitter disappointment that my dreams of love with his man are shattered.

He knows the gig is up.

As I slowly approach the curb at the airline terminal, he's still promising to pay me back the $2,500 that he charged on my credit card—*with my consent*. At this point, I know it will never happen. I just want him out of my car. I watch him walk away, thankful that he's out of my life yet feeling the full impact of the imposter love he had professed.

The deception settles on my heart and mind like a dark, ominous cloud right before it rains. On the way home, my cell phone rings. It's him. He blurts out that he needs more money because his credit card is not working, and he can't pay for his flight. The only thing I say is, "NO!" as I hit the hang up button extra hard. I never hear from him again except for one text a week later where he tells me to watch my back.

Dealing with My Heartbreak

My heart is fractured into a million pieces yet it's not really the money I have to pay back that bothers me so much. It's that I believed it was the real thing…true love. A future with a loving mate. A mutually nurturing, caring relationship.

As I usually do in the flight, flee, freeze, or fawn response, I crawl into my impenetrable emotional tent and zip up the zipper. I withdraw. I isolate. I cocoon. I must process what just happened and I need to be alone.

Over the next few months as I process the relationship illusion and attempt to absorb the scourge of scorn from those around me, I wonder how I missed the signposts and warning flags. I ponder how I'm going to reclaim my heart. How can I ever trust the intents of a man again after being intentionally deceived? Should I just give up on love because trusting is too painful? What books can I read that will repair the damage of having my heart swindled?

For me, the Bible holds the answers, as it always does, for those who seek its truth. I spend long hours studying and meditating in the book of Psalms and Proverbs. I pray for God to heal my heart, to reclaim it wholly as His own. Not that I had lost it, but a part of it had been misused… stolen. I grieve the loss of a dream I thought was coming true—*the love of potential*, which I'll explain a little later. I journal. I talk to close, trusted friends. I read. I even pray for the perpetuator, that he would realize he had messed with one of God's daughters, and that he would stop doing the same thing to other women. Unfortunately, that was not the case. I've personally met three of his ex-wives. I am one of the fortunate ones who escaped marrying him.

I accept my part in the illusion (not doing my homework and identifying my personal gaps that may have contributed to the initial lure) when I realize that this one incident will not define my future. When I fully embrace the fact that I'm worthy and deserving of the genuine, consistent love of a man, and, more importantly, when I step fully into who I am as a woman…F-i-n-a-l-l-y…my heart is reclaimed!

To be clear, the stories in this book didn't simply *happen* to the women—we each fully participated in the illusion. At the genesis of each relationship, we had no reason to think the love we were being offered *wasn't* real. But at some point, and everyone has their point, when we were finally brave enough to exit the situation, a plethora of emotions cascaded over us in the following months and years. We felt shame. We felt self-blame. We felt angry that someone felt entitled to rope us into their realm and that we did not notice the signs earlier. We felt twinges of depression as we recalibrated our soul back to normalcy.

When something like this happens to you, people judge you. They fully believe in their hearts that this could NEVER happen to them. Some will think less of you. Others will think you're gullible, even stupid, for falling for a full-on narcissist, future faker, or romance scammer. They'll question, "Didn't you see the signs?" When you're the one in it, you can honestly say, no you didn't…not at first anyway. Even those closest to us may have noticed a few initial red flags yet felt hesitant to share their observations because they were overjoyed to see our happiness…and we probably wouldn't have listened anyway.

What many don't realize is that you can do all the Google searching you want but it most often doesn't reveal the ill intent of a person, nor if they have a personality disorder. Even though it wasn't a romance scam, I can't help but wonder how the thousands of Bernie Madoff Ponzi scheme subjects felt when they realized they'd been duped by a pro.

The stories in this book are based on true events. The circumstances these women endured really did happen, even though the names, places, and surrounding details have been changed for obvious reasons. When I first got the idea, I approached a handful of women in my inner circle to see if they'd be willing to share their journey and all of them said yes. Once I started telling women in my outer circle about the title and subtitle, a few very willingly offered to share their story, first, because it hadn't yet been told to the public, and second, because it provided further healing for their heart. My purpose for writing this book is to educate women on how a *narcissist, future faker, romance scammer, or intimacy anorexia predator* sets up their lie to rope women in and in the 10 Red Flags section you'll learn how to spot them quickly.

To get the most from this book, you can either read it start to finish, or based on the titles in the Table of Contents, you can skip to the stories that you relate to the most. I suggest that you capture the thoughts that speak loudly and directly to your heart. I've included four Personal Reflection blank pages in the back of the book to jot down your emotions or thoughts as you read.

If you haven't experienced any of the scenarios this book contains, you could be doing a close relative, friend, or co-worker the biggest favor of their lives by gifting them this book.

At the end of each woman's chronicle are the hard earned, priceless *Heroic Heartbeat Lessons* on what she learned during and after her journey. Read with care because their lessons will help you, too. Please note that I will not use the word *victim* in this book as I believe it's disempowering on many levels.

The Love of Potential

I believe the reason why women fall for Liars, Losers, and Lunatics is *the love of potential*. A good friend of mine describes it *as fantasizing or falling in love with the idea of someone—the idea of who they could be and who you want them to ideally be for you in your life, but it ultimately is not who they really are.*

Since the *love of potential* is not a term most of us are familiar with, I'll take a moment to share my own interpretation of what I believe it means. Embracing the *love of potential* is like stepping into a world of enchantment, where women are captivated by the possibilities they see in a potential suitor. I envision a fairy tale romance with a happy ending. I then embark on a journey filled with the allure of what could be, a grand love story that echoes through time, much like the ones we adore in romantic dramas. Even when challenges arise, a woman with the *love of potential* believes in a mutual love that can conquer everything life puts in front of her and her partner.

I understand the trauma and confusion that targets of romance scams experience. It's an incredibly difficult situation to be in, and something that can leave deep emotional and financial scars. My hope is that this book will help raise awareness and provide support for those affected. By reading stories from survivors of romance scams, future fakers, and narcissistic abuse, I trust you will gain a new empathy and offer support and understanding to those who have been affected.

I'm confident that sharing stories from survivors will help prevent potential targets from falling prey to these scams. It's important to keep in mind that the people behind these scams are often sophisticated and manipulative, so it's essential to stay vigilant and be aware of the warning signs and sometimes subtle red flags.

While I was writing this book, I put out a query to a sourcing website and was contacted by a former long-time CEO of an online dating site. This is what he shared with me:

> "We constantly updated our site to safeguard our users, but it still wasn't enough to stop scammers. The most common scam we saw was a fake profile being created, using photos of attractive men or women that were downloaded from other sites. One Swedish modeling agency took precautions to block downloads and placed a warning on their model's photos. Once the fake profile goes live then the scammer will try to engage and ask the target to communicate via WhatsApp or similar. This is because their inappropriate activity would soon be spotted or reported, and the fake profile deleted by the dating site company.
>
> "Once the scammer establishes communication, they will talk about things that appeal to their target and arrange a meeting. The basic scammer will ask you to help them with travel expenses, making a variety of excuses why they cannot pay themselves. These are usually lone operators and small-time scammers based in other countries.

"The most advanced scammers are extremely organized and are based in countries such as Russia. They operate a shift system so the person you think you are chatting with is always available. They will engage with you over a period of weeks, even months, and they are most likely talking to multiple targets. They create a fake family and will send you photos of recent holidays and birthday parties. If you ask to have a phone or video call, they will usually decline while providing a reasonable sounding excuse. This is the first warning sign. Check the photos for anything suspicious such as if they say they are a Russian living in the United States, look at simple things like if the plug sockets in their home are US or European. If they send a photo with cars, look at the vehicle number plates and road signs from the country they claim to be living in.

"The sophisticated scammer does not ask for money. They will claim to be a professional investor and once they have your confidence, they will offer to help *you* make money. They may tell you they deal in gold or gems and can get you a great deal. Never give your credit card details to them or enter a site they ask you to view.

"In conclusion, the rule of thumb is if they will not talk on the phone or meet for a coffee, it's a scam. If they do meet or chat with you on the phone, you should still never give your new friend your bank or credit card details, or loan them money, no matter how dire they say their situation appears. If you refuse and they are a scammer they will soon disappear."

Five Primary Types of Romantic Deceivers

Before we get into our first story, let's look at the definition of the five primary types of predators, whether in person or online. And, by the way, predators don't skulk only on dating sites, they prey in person, too!

Narcissistic Abuse

According to [1]Medical News Today, "Narcissistic abuse is **a form of abuse stemming from narcissistic behaviors**. It can be emotional, psychological, or physical. Narcissistic characteristics can include volatile behavior, lack of empathy, and aggression. Narcissistic abuse may include gaslighting, constant criticism, humiliation, and coercion." The narcissist has an inflated view of their self-importance, an amplified need for attention and admiration, controlling behaviors, manipulative tactics, and lack of empathy. The typical pattern of a narcissist is idealization (includes love bombing and making you feel like you're on a pedestal), devaluing (withdrawing

---

[1] Medical News Today. What is Narcissistic Abuse and What Are the Signs? https://www.medicalnewstoday.com. https://www.medicalnewstoday.com/articles/narcissistic-abuse. Accessed on August 5, 2023.

affection or withholding emotional or physical intimacy) and discarding (insults may worsen if you no longer give the narcissist the emotional "high" they need as it's imperative that the narcissist becomes the "winner" in the relationship).

Future Faking

According to New York City based psychologist, Greg Kushick, PsyD, as he told [2]health.com, "Future faking is when someone uses a detailed vision of the future to facilitate the bonding and connection in a romantic relationship." Future faking is a manipulative strategy often used by narcissists to get what they want from you in the present moment. For instance, did you ever start dating someone who made lavish promises of trips and gifts at the beginning of your relationship that never materialized? If yes, then you've experienced future faking.

Fantasist: According to [3]Collins Dictionary, a Fantasist is "someone who constantly tells lies about their life and achievements in order to make themselves sound more exciting than they really are."

---

[2] Health.com. All About 'Future Faking': A Dating Strategy Used by Narcissists. https://www.health.com. https://www.health.com/relationships/future-faking

[3] Collins Dictionary. https://www.collinsdictionary.com. https://www.collinsdictionary.com/dictionary/english/fantasist.

Romance Scams

According to the fbi.gov website, "Romance scams occur when a criminal adopts a fake online identity to gain a survivor's affection and trust. The scammer then uses the illusion of a romantic or close relationship to manipulate and/or steal from the survivor."

Intimacy Anorexia Predator

Honestly, I hadn't even heard of this term until I started marketing this book. A friend from high school way back in the day sent me an article by psychologist, Dr. Doug Weiss, who coined the term. Although not a formally recognized condition, Dr. Weiss describes this type of predator as someone who first love bombs and then actively and intentionally withholds emotional, spiritual, and sexual intimacy from a partner. This is just another way for the perpetrator to gain control and manipulation over their target.

PART I

LIARS

1

THE DUTIFUL WIFE AND GIRLFRIEND

"Trust yourself, trust your gut, and test your gut."

I was twenty-four when I met Mitch online. We talked to each other at length every day on the phone and it seemed like we were connecting well on an intellectual and emotional level. I hadn't made a mental note at the time, but Mitch spent considerable time telling me all the things his ex-fiancé did wrong to keep me in line, to make sure I didn't do those things. Thinking I was a dutiful girlfriend, I was careful to fall in line with his expectations. Three months passed, and I had to leave for the summer to go back to college, but he traveled to where I was staying. After two weeks of being together in person, I was surprised when Mitch proposed.

Mitch had asked my parents for my hand in marriage before he proposed. On the day he proposed, my parents waited anxiously for a call. The call never came because Mitch had a specific way he wanted the scenario to play out, which was different from the proposal he'd made with an ex-fiancé. Apparently, I had blasted out the news to everyone and their mother and there was so much hub bub that they didn't get to celebrate as they, or he, wanted. In their anxiousness, my parents finally called me to ask if it had happened yet. What resulted from how Mitch wanted it to play out, was that it placed him as a priority above my family. I noticed that an initial isolation and discord started to take root within me toward my mom.

During that time in my life my mom was very controlling and was sowing guilt into me because I clearly saw what was happening, and as a result, I tried to hold on tighter. At the time, I didn't understand her communication style, so every interaction with her drove me further into Mitch's arms. He capitalized on the situation by reiterating that he was right and that my mom was crazy.

Only a brief time after Mitch and I were married, we began to have issues. It seemed as if I were constantly making mental notes about what topics not to broach, especially in front of others. I remember we were looking for a place to live, so Mitch and I and my parents were in the car together on a house hunt. My perpetual "job" was to play goalie: *remember, Jenevieve, don't make him mad, don't bring up that subject. Keep my parents at bay so they don't say something to upset him.* If I didn't abide by Mitch's rules, and my parents said something to offend him, he would tell me later how crappy my family was.

The peculiar thing was that he held a ton of respect for my dad, perhaps because Mitch didn't have a dad.

Time progressed and Mitch became more aggressive with keeping me in line. First, it was isolation, the divide and conquer tactics with my family, but then he started to tell me areas where I was stupid, where I was worthless. Looking back on it, he was so subtle that I didn't notice he was even doing it because his verbal attacks were more like back-handed compliments, "Well, you have great legs, you should work out more." I had started gaining weight as I headed into my thirties because I had a husband who couldn't love me, and my self-esteem was plummeting.

My perpetual task was to make sure that Mitch was never uncomfortable. He moved to Mankato before I did because I was finishing my last year in college. He'd call me with hurtful messages like, "I'm falling for somebody at work because you're never around." Under that guise, one time a group of fellow college students and I had taken a train from Chicago back to Minneapolis on a school trip and I drove forty-five minutes that same night all the way to Mankato after an exhausting weekend. I got home at 2 a.m. in the morning because I was petrified he was going to cheat on me. Mitch had told me he had plans with the woman the next day, so I felt like I had to be there to foil the plan. Turns out he was lying. He often told lies to get what he wanted, or as manipulation to get what he wanted out of me.

Over time, things that would not normally upset me would make me angry simply because *he* was angry. I realized years later that I was a mirror—anything that upset Mitch, upset me, yet I was the one who appeared crazy. I remember one time putting my foot through a wall because I was mad at something that had made him mad. I would yell at the Filipino neighbors who lived above us and who often cooked at 2 a.m., 3 a.m., 4 a.m. in the morning, yet sounded more like they were bowling with 300-pound bowling balls. I would stomp like a wild woman upstairs and flip out on them. Mitch never did. Just me. He exerted such an intense amount of control over the situation—and me—he didn't have to be the crazy one.

Once divorce seemed inevitable, I went through the house and tore all the pictures off the wall. Mitch called the police and told them I was the crazy one wreaking havoc in our home. Since Mitch was Catholic, we finally went to see the priest. Mitch had told me that we were not *really* married because he was Catholic, and I wasn't. It was that Catholic priest who saw through him. We had been to multiple therapy sessions with a multitude of therapists and none of them could see through him. If they called him out on anything specific, he just wouldn't go back.

I remember calling the priest the night Mitch called the police. I told him matter-of-factly, "I punched him." The priest responded, "Don't you think God would say that you've had enough?" By the time I called the priest, it had gotten to the point where I was hiding in closets when Mitch came home because I wasn't sure what kind of mood he would be in. I'd wait to come out if I sensed it was a *safe* day. Even our dog feared him. It was in the conversation with the priest that day that helped me to walk away. I had always been taught that divorce wasn't an option; that you stay until death do you part except in the case of adultery or physical abuse.

The only reason I was capable and able to leave was because Mitch had already set his sights on somebody else and had been cheating on me. The weekend before I left, Mitch said he had to go on a business trip, which wasn't a business trip at all. He had gone to see her, and I discovered later that that's the weekend she got pregnant. He came back home on Sunday night, and on Monday, June 18th, my mom rented an 18-foot trailer so when Mitch got on the bus to go to work, we emptied the house.

My mom later told me that she knew what Mitch was all about on our wedding day. He told her on our wedding day to sit down and shut up, and that I didn't have anything to do with her anymore. That I *had* to cut her out. The December before I left, I told my mom that I was done with her—per Mitch, I wasn't allowed to speak to her, although I continued to have conversations with my dad. My mom had loudly and consistently voiced her resolve to get me out of the marriage, but I knew it had to be my decision. Looking back, I was extremely fortunate to have parents, godparents, and friends around me who pulled me out of the burning building of an abusive marriage.

After Mitch saw that I'd taken everything, and that I had left him with two lawn chairs because everything else was mine, he called in a rage, "What is this? You left me with lawn chairs?" I responded, "If you contact me again there will be a restraining order placed against you." That scared him enough, because he was always concerned about living within the law, whether it was a law of his religion or the law of the government. He did try to friend me on Facebook in 2015 or 2016. Inwardly, I thought, *good riddance, dude. I don't know who you think you are.*

And then one day in 2019 I received a text message from his wife, "You don't know me, but..." "I knew exactly who it was. "...I'm reaching out to apologize for cheating on you. When I got involved with Mitch, I had no idea he was married. And by the time I figured it out, I had already bought into it all." I realized a year and a half after their baby was born that I was in a dire situation. Now, thirteen years and six kids later, I continued the text, "I need to know, am I seeing what I think I'm seeing or am I as crazy as he says I am?" Knowing full well what she was going through, I reached out and had a conversation with her, "You're seeing what you think you're seeing. You are not crazy." He had been telling her that *I* was a narcissist.

I asked, "Have you heard the word narcissist before?"

"Yeah, he tells me I'm a narcissist all the time."

I said, "I need you to look that up. Will you please look that up when we get off the phone? Because this is what you're dealing with."

She asked me to forgive her.

I had been reading a book called *Red Moon Rising: How 24-7 Prayer Is Awakening a Generation* by Pete Greig and Dave Roberts. That book helped me to forgive and move on, so I shared with her, "I forgave you years ago, and I've been praying for you even from the beginning that you wouldn't be abused the way I was."

She couldn't believe that I could do that.

"That's what being a Christian is about."

If I didn't forgive, I would have carried the baggage around with me. Something important to remember if you've been the survivor of a narcissistic abuser: if you don't get the help you need you will continue to pull the same type of people into your life, because you continue to choose it for yourself. There is an aspect of who you are that narcissists are attracted to, and if you can't see the red flags, you *choose* to allow it.

I quit dating for five years because men with narcissistic personalities were all I seemed to attract. The very last person I talked to several times on the phone with, and went on one date with, I clearly saw the red flags of narcissism, and ran. That same day, I called my mom and proclaimed in the most excited voice, "I just had the worst date of my life!"

My mom was like, "You sound excited about that."

"I am because I see the red flags now and I will never let it happen again because now I trust myself."

It's worth doing the work!

Heroic Heartbeat Lessons

- Enlist the help of a therapist. A trusted pastor. A coach. An executive coach. Seek out someone to help you work through the necessary mindset shifts so you understand what you're doing to pull these people into your life. Because chances are, it's not just men. Chances are you have family members, co-workers, bosses, church members, friends, and others in your sphere with narcissistic tendencies who you're attracting.

- Find somebody who's whole, who's doing the work themselves, and ask them to be your mentor, your guide through the process. If you're not doing the work, you're only going to keep attracting people who are unhealthy, you're not going to see it coming.

And, chances are, if there's nobody else around you to abuse you, you turn inward and you start to abuse yourself if you haven't done the work. When God was in the process of yanking me out of my former self, it was a wrestling match. I thought I was simply being who I was…a kind, thoughtful, nurturing person. Although I did embody those positive traits, I was still caught in self-abuse. When I ultimately found myself married to a wonderful, loving man and working for a company that supported me on every level, I fell back into the old pattern of believing I was worthless.

- A key steppingstone is when you wake up to that blind spot and discover that there's no need to abuse yourself anymore because you're emotionally healthy, that's when true transformation takes place.

- Trust yourself, trust your gut, and test your gut. If you notice yellow or red flags, face those flags and bring them to somebody you trust implicitly. They know you and can help clear the fog that sometimes muddles our minds when we meet someone new. When you've been through a narcissistic abuse situation and make strong mental notes of the red flags, if it happens again, you'll see the red flags a lot faster.

- Lastly, don't head into relationships at light speed. Narcissistic abusers will tell you everything that you don't tell yourself. It's like they read the needs in you. They rope you in quickly to gain power and control. If you're waiting for somebody else to make you happy, you may as well throw in the towel now because you will never be happy. Do the work so you are whole and remember there is no one who can make you whole besides God.

2

GOTTA WATCH OUT FOR THOSE ONLINE DATING SCAMS!

This chapter is a short collection of stories from women who are survivors of online dating scams.

I was the victim of an online dating scam in 2005. At the time, I was naive to scams and didn't expect what would happen to me.

First, the scammer hooked me emotionally by being attentive, loving, and kind through emails and phone calls. He said he was an engineer and had a young daughter. When I continued to suggest that we meet in person, he used excuse after excuse to put it off until finally he told me he was going to Spain so his daughter could have stem cell surgery for a grave illness. He kept in touch by phone while he was supposedly in Spain. During one conversation, I heard loud banging in the background and the phone went dead. I panicked about what might have happened. My mind was going crazy because I thought he and his daughter were in some kind of danger.

I called my brother who had kept telling me from the beginning that this man was a scam artist. My brother was a homicide detective and knew well the nature of shady people. I felt trapped between fantasy and reality, and my heart wouldn't allow me to step over the line into reality. After all, this supposed engineer man had said he loved me and wanted to be with me. He must have sensed my loneliness and desire for a meaningful relationship.

Finally, the scammer told me that robbers had stolen all his money for the stem cell operation and his trip back to New York, and at that point, and with my brother's help, I knew the guy was a scammer. I had finally stepped into reality.

Heroic Heartbeat Lessons

- During this experience I learned that most scammers possess very distinguishable traits. They claim to be widowers, have a child, and usually have an occupation that will take them out of the country.
- They usually get stranded overseas and ask for money, usually in the form of an iTunes card or some kind of untraceable form of monetary exchange.

- If you do a search on their phone number it will always be unlisted, since they'll have acquired an untraceable Google phone number.

I met "the predator" on a dating app. He was good-looking, athletic, and adventurous; qualities that instantly attracted me to him. He was extremely charming and took me out to expensive restaurants and other venues, all of which I enjoyed. I thought *maybe this is "the one."*

The predator wined and dined me for a few months before he asked about borrowing money. He sounded convincing about the investment opportunities he was working on and shared about how I could help him close the deal by advancing some money. I started seeing his true intentions when borrowing money became a routine. He was always sweet and charming just before asking for money. Initially, I gave him some money, but quickly realized that he was a scammer. Whenever I asked him about his job or investments, he was vague with his answers and talked in circles, so I never really understood what he was talking about.

Heroic Heartbeat Lessons

- I learned not to be so easily trusting. Just because someone *sounds* sincere, that's no reason to give them anything, especially money.

- I learned to trust my gut. If it doesn't feel right, it probably isn't.
- If it seems too good to be true, it probably is.

After I was divorced, my kids created a Facebook profile for me and taught me the fundamentals of using it. They said it would help us stay in touch and let me see pictures of my grandchildren. One day, a service member serving in Afghanistan on a peacekeeping mission sent me a friend request. Doug invited me to be his Facebook friend, so I made the decision to accept it. Our relationship didn't begin as a romantic relationship, although he claimed he was lonely and looking for companionship while on duty in the middle of nowhere.

Soon after becoming friends, Doug revealed to me that his wife had passed away from cancer and that his experience caring for her was identical to my own when my spouse also succumbed to the disease. He emailed me photos that I eventually realized were taken from the internet. One day he declared that his time in the American military was almost up but that he was being posted to Nigeria. He constantly expressed his eagerness for our union, and we grew quite close as we began emailing daily because he said emailing was more convenient than using Facebook.

Doug claimed to appreciate gemstones and expressed his desire to own a jewelry store when he retired. Because he was close to the precious stone mines and could purchase them for a very low price, he claimed that this was the best aspect of living in Nigeria. After telling me he was coming to see me, he told me he had a problem getting money to pay for an export tax on his jewels because his bank card wasn't accepted in Nigeria. I sent him some cash to pay the tax, which he stated was only 2% of the worth of the diamonds yet amounted to $15,000 in total.

I knew it was a lot of money to give, but I reasoned that if things worked out, I would spend the rest of my life with this good and honest serviceman. The situation was okay up until his layover in Malaysia. The jewels allegedly were taken by customs authorities, who then demanded cash to release them. This time, the price was $20,000 I explained to him that I had to borrow against the family mortgage and that it would take some time to get the money.

Still believing Doug was a legit man, and not ever having dealt with a con artist, I transferred the money to Malaysian officials, but I was informed that I needed to speak with Doug's attorney because Doug was now being held in jail for smuggling. The attorney advised him that obtaining an anti-terrorism and money-laundering certificate would cost an additional $10,000 and added that an additional $5,000 would be needed to cover Doug's legal fees as well as his own.

I sent the funds, but afterwards, Doug claimed that a different government official had demanded payment so he could extend his visa while he awaited the court to review all the paperwork. He contacted me almost daily with a new request for money. Different officials within various Malaysian government entities sent me formal certifications, documents to complete, and invoices for everything. I had the impression that Malaysia's entire government was corrupt. I'm not sure precisely how much I sent, but it was more than $100,000. Money wasn't important to me. I genuinely believed Doug would repay me for helping him; therefore I only wanted to help him get out of this jam.

I continued to receive demands even after I ran out of money. Indecisive as to what to do, I eventually contacted the police. They confirmed that my encounter had many elements in common with a dating and romance scam and that it was highly unlikely I would get any of my money back. Even now, I can't help but feel guilty about disappointing Doug, even though I know in my head it was all a con.

Heroic Heartbeat Lessons

- At the first sign of money being involved, stop! Say no, no matter how dire the situation seems.
- If they can't abide by your terms regarding communication method, run!
- No real man will allow a woman to "save" him from an overseas emergency.
- Never, ever, take out a loan or borrow from your mortgage to help a man who says he's staying or living in another country.

PART II

LOSERS

3

FUTURE FAKERS

*"I learned not to dive so fast into relationships.
Take time, spend time, talk to the person, and then
let them talk and talk and talk."*

I was living my life as I always did. Predictable. Orderly. Never boring. I thrive on organization, routine, and structure. Always have.

My days are filled with gym time five to six days a week, daily devotional time in the Bible and prayer, the bulk of my workdays spent working on and in my business, and then my evening routine. This year (2023) counts twenty-three years of being divorced…the same amount of time I was married.

I love living life on my own terms, according to my carefully crafted schedule and body rhythms. To me, that's success, or at least *my* definition of success. I love my freedom of time and place a high value on it.

My faith in God permeates every area of my life and even though I sin and fail on a regular basis, I depend on Jesus to lead and guide my every step, every decision, every thought, word, and deed. The first thing I do each morning is thank God that He woke me up and then ask Him to help me fulfill the reason why He woke me up. My overarching desire is that God would keep me in the very center of His will and purpose for my life. That's a big deal to me.

I am content with living alone. At this stage of life at sixty-six, I kinda feel like it's my destiny to be single due to a string of disappointing relationships over the years. In the past, it seemed as if men either wanted to control me or criticize me. They mistook my kindness for weakness but when they realized the depth of my inner strength, they didn't stick around long. I always wondered why; like *why wouldn't you want a strong, independent woman?* But weak, broken men don't want that—they want to dominate and control because they gain some sense of strength by doing so. Truthfully, I don't trust myself to make wise decisions about men anymore. Besides, many men my age seem so old and couch potato-ish. Of course, this is a generalization, not all men my age are like that. Some are dynamos; active and energetic, but I digress.

I was a late bloomer so now in my mid-sixties I look young for my years, although when I look in the mirror, I notice the gray hairs coming through yet again and I ask myself *why those stubborn grays grow back so fast.* Besides the gray hair and a few wrinkles, which I consider badges of honor, I feel vibrant and energetic.

My sense of stability jetted to outer space one Saturday morning while I was at the gym. I noticed a handsome medium-toned man with a mustache on an exercise bike. I continued my workout and was headed from a cable machine to another exercise when we first crossed paths. He smiled at me, lifted one side of his headphones and said matter-of-factly, "Nice form." Feeling a spark of attraction, I smiled back, and said, "Why, thank you!" When I returned home, I immediately called my friend Laura and exclaimed with excitement, "I met a handsome brutha at the gym this morning!" We both giggled like schoolgirls for a few moments and then moved on to another conversation, but I didn't forget the handsome *gym man*. Every Saturday, I strategically timed my gym visits with anticipation of seeing him again and perhaps crossing paths.

Then one Saturday in late January, it happened.

From the elliptical trainer I was warming up on, I spotted him! There he was, gym man, at his usual place on one of the stationary bikes. We exchanged a quick mutual smile as I darted off to start my workout. I wasn't planning to do legs that day but in my quest to get a better look, I conveniently positioned myself on a seated leg press machine directly across from the stationary bike he was on. It was a deliberate move to get his attention, although I pretended to put on my serious "don't mess with me" gym face and acted like I was totally into the press machine.

I heard a voice behind me. "Happy new year!" he exclaimed. I turned and the spark ignited. "Well happy new year to you, too!" We struck up a conversation, and after a couple minutes of casual chit chat, he didn't waste any time asking for my phone number. It was the NFL playoff season and he suggested that we meet and watch a game together. As a serious football fan, I was overjoyed and replied with enthusiasm, "YES, that would be great!" I learned his name was Kendrick. We talked for several more minutes and I left the gym that morning with a gigantic smile on my face and walking two inches off the ground...at least that's the way I felt. *Man is he handsome*, I thought, *and* nicely put together. *Who says women aren't visual?* I was giddy with excitement at the thought of meeting Kendrick to watch football as his charismatic demeanor made him easy to talk to.

Within an hour of leaving the gym, I received a text from him telling me that I had a great smile and to keep smiling. *Aaaaaah, how sweet*, I thought after my initial muse of *wow, that was fast*. I called one of my inner circle friends and shouted out, "Hey, I have a date next week with a handsome brutha!"

The night of the second round of the NFL playoffs came and my Dallas Cowboys were part of the mix. I felt a twinge of nervousness as I settled into a high-top at a local sports tavern while I waited for Kendrick. Once there, we immediately leapt into a spirited conversation. He talked about his life as a former K9 police officer and regaled me with stories of his on-duty activities, including killing several drug-induced or violent assailants in the line of duty. I found myself captivated by his stories, and by his confidence and charm.

After the playoff first date, we were supposed to meet somewhere for a second date, but I ended up having a relapse of a bad flu I had had during Thanksgiving. Kendrick had two large containers of soup delivered to me from a local restaurant and I was amazed at his thoughtfulness, but it didn't stop there. He called multiple times to check on how I was feeling. When I recovered, he brought me a dozen gourmet mini cupcakes on Valentine's Day. They were decadent as I indulged in one each day until they were history! I was reveling in his wonderful attention and nurturing.

Shortly after the cupcakes we decided to go for a roasted lamb dinner on that upcoming Saturday. But we had waited too long. The upscale restaurants who served lamb were all booked. Ah ha…solution! I bragged to Kendrick that I could *throw down* in the kitchen and that I would cook a mean lamb dinner for him. A day later, he went to Trader Joe's and bought a Frenched rack of lamb with special seasoning an employee assured him would be perfect, a bag of basmati rice, baby asparagus, and a nice bottle of pinot noir, which he delivered at my door in an insulated Trader Joe's red and black cloth tote bag the next morning at 7 a.m. "Oh my gosh," I proclaimed, "Wow, what is all this? On Sunday, I cooked a wonderful lamb dinner and we feasted royally.

Our first real "date" consisted of meeting at Bonefish Grill. He went on and on about how great I looked and how much he loved what I was wearing. Like on and ON and ON. I had never had a man gush over me like that before, or for that long. After we ate, we went to a movie of his choice, had ice-cream afterward, and ate a slice of pizza later in the evening. We held hands and it felt like they fit together like a glove—so natural—I hadn't held hands out in public with anyone in a long time.

During that first month of seeing each other, Kendrick showered me with attention, compliments, and promises of trips to exotic locales, most…no…all of which were going to "be a surprise." He'd start out verbally planning and then interrupt himself, "No, just wait, it's going to be a surprise." He once asked me if I liked diamonds to which I replied, "I hear they're a girl's best friend." Anything I'd say I liked, he'd say, "Done," as if it was really going to happen. We'd walk past luggage in a department store, and he'd ask, "Do you like that?"

"Sure."

"I'll have it sent to you."

He bought me a pair of cheap sunglasses at a mall kiosk and told me I looked like Jackie O in them, all the while promising to buy me an expensive pair *one day*. I wasn't catching the signs of a future faker, not knowing what that even was. After all, he seemed so sincere, so genuine. He told me, "I want to give you everything!" All our conversations were *about the future*. He had indicated he wanted to talk about our past relationship hurts and other serious topics, but it was always slated as *a future conversation*.

His grand gesture was a trip to Florence, Italy…*in the future*, of course. Oh yes, we were going to stay at the St. Regis because he only traveled first class and stayed at top-rate hotels. Right. We were going to take a day trip to Venice and another day trip to Rome. We watched tons of YouTube videos on things to do in Florence and other cities. He said the day we left, one of his private drivers would come to pick me up and that all I had to do was show up at the airport and he would manage the rest. I thought this was grand as women usually have to do all the planning.

I have to say that from the beginning of our relationship, I heard the still, small voice of the Holy Spirit whispering, or I should say shouting in my spirit, *Guard your heart with all diligence.* I didn't perceive that it was the Holy Spirit's prompting at first, but I heard it often and it ultimately made sense.

Another Sunday when Kendrick was over, he brought out a rectangle box of seven mini fragrances and told me to pick my top three favorites. We went one by one as I sniffed and made my selections. He told me the one I picked was $450 an ounce and that he would...*in the future*...buy me some for my birthday or other special occasion. I shared this experience with my inner-circle long-time male friend, and he immediately laughed and said, "Take it from a former womanizer, that perfume is classic player paraphernalia!" I couldn't believe my ears.

As our relationship progressed, I started making mental notes about Kendrick and his behavior. We texted daily, often several times a day, at first. He'd call me during the day just to say hello and tell me he just wanted to hear my voice, and then we would talk every evening. At first, Kendrick said he went to bed super early but as time marched on, he would call me later and later, saying he was on the highway driving home. When I'd asked him specific questions about his life, he'd answer vaguely or talked in circles.

One Friday about a month in, he didn't text or call the entire day, which wasn't his "pattern." The next day when I questioned him about why he *ghosted* me, he replied that he was a conservative Black man and he didn't know what ghosting was; mind you, he never answered the question as to why he hadn't made his nightly call. He ghosted me the next night as well except for a generic "Enjoy your evening" text at ten o'clock. I tried to brush off my concerns, but they lingered in the back of my mind. By this time, he alluded in a text that he loved me, although he didn't say it directly. He said, "I feel it." I texted back, "What are you talking about?" He immediately called me, but not before he texted "May I call you?" He always asked permission to call to make himself *appear* like a gentleman. I liked it because no one had ever done that before. That night we both said "I love you" over the phone.

The thing is, he never said I love you while looking into my eyes. He either texted it, told me over the phone, or when he was halfway out the door. I was telling him "I love you too," but he'd never make eye contact, which I thought was strange. A couple of weeks before this, he told me, again in a text, that he bet the time would come when I would tell him I loved him. I was taking everything at face value so there was no reason to look for or notice a red flag. Once when we went out for an early dinner, although we had a good time, when I got back home, I felt an uneasiness settling into my spirit, although I couldn't place it at the time. I texted one of my inner-circle friends and said, "Something doesn't feel right."

Kendrick was secretive about his life, career, and daily schedule, and he never picked me up for our dates. He requested that I meet him at a predetermined location, even if it was five minutes away. I pushed the issue a couple of times and he simply replied that he was on call. I couldn't shake the feeling that something wasn't right. I wondered if I was being paranoid or if my unsettled feelings were justified.

At one point, I was convinced, and still am, that Kendrick had bugged my living room because I would mention things when I talked with friends, and next thing I knew, he would address the same subject. That happened more than a few times. It got to the point where when I wanted to talk to my inner circle friends, I'd barricade myself in the upstairs bathroom of my house. I'd stuff a bathmat underneath the door to muffle the sound. I told a friend of mine that the fact that I even felt the need to barricade myself in my bathroom with a mat under the door was cause for concern.

One day, Kendrick dropped a bombshell on me. He said he had been diagnosed with cancer. At first, I sat in silence, and then true to my conversation style, I asked a ton of questions—I communicated that I was committed to supporting him in any way I could. But there were things about his diagnosis that didn't add up. I started to suspect that Kendrick was lying to me. He sat on my living room couch one Sunday with REAL TEARS pooling under his eyes and his head in his hands.

As he sat silent for several minutes, I sat next to him with one hand on his back in my attempt to reassure him. Earlier I had asked him if he were hungry and told him that I could air fry some Italian sausage to which he declined, saying he was too distraught. Once the tears subsided, I asked him again if he was hungry. He said yes this time and ended up eating THREE Italian sausages wrapped in sourdough bread and slathered with spicy mustard. I thought *ummmm, that's pretty good for not wanting to eat just an hour before.*

Every single time he came over on Sunday, he'd leave by 5pm. Later that evening, I left him a voice note telling him I would stand with him during his treatment and that I wasn't going anywhere. That's when the communication stopped...completely. The next morning, I sent him a good morning text and four hours later I received a good morning reply. That was my cue that he was not into me or our relationship any longer. No calls. No texts. Two months and it had run its course—Kendrick's mission was accomplished. The emotional manipulation was complete: a woman had said she loved him and pledged her devotion to care for him during his health storm. I've not heard from him since.

After communication stopped, I reached out to a friend of mine who is a former private investigator to get his thoughts on the situation. I explained the circumstances: the leaving early on Sundays, the meeting in separate cars…all the clues I had gathered in the short two months. The first thing from my friend's mouth was, "Sounds like he's married." He told me to pay for an online investigative service to do some deeper digging, which I did. Oh, my word, the information I discovered! Kendrick told me he had signed over the house to his ex-wife in their divorce. Uh, NO! Records showed that he and his wife…yes, his CURRENT wife had sold their house to another couple in 2019 AND they currently have the same address at the apartment where he lives. No quit claim deed, which would have had to be in place had he signed over the house. I gathered all kinds of information about him and his family.

In the aftermath, I felt like I was experiencing something like the stages of death or loss. At first, I was in disbelief about what I had discovered about Kendrick. Then I got angry—angry at him for thinking it was okay to mess with an innocent Christian woman, angry at myself for falling for manipulative trickery. Slight depression took over for several days as I processed the illusion that I had been a part of, believing it was true. I finally came to realize that I had gleaned valuable life lessons through the experience.

I spent hours researching narcissistic behavior and master manipulators, trying to understand how I could have fallen for Kendrick's tricks. Amid my investigating, I also researched narcissistic behavior and *future faking*, a term I hadn't heard before. I talked with others who had dealt with master manipulators. I learned that they often use grand gestures and promises of luxury vacations and gifts to gain emotional control over their survivors. I felt a sense of relief knowing that I wasn't alone in my experience. I gained a sense of empowerment as I learned more about common predator tactics and how to protect myself.

I also learned that manipulators can be extremely skilled at hiding their true selves, and that it can take months or even years for their survivors to realize what's really going on. Even though the person has exited your life, the aftermath continues to mess with your psyche. At times I feel like I'm being watched from a distance or that he's lurking in the gym parking lot.

In the end, I realized that I was a survivor of a master manipulator, a future faker, who used his charm and lies to gain control over me. I also learned to trust my intuition and not ignore the warning signs.

I felt embarrassed for telling so many people about my new "boyfriend." It had been eight years since the ex-fiancé debacle, and in the beginning, I was excited at the prospect of love—*the love of potential*. What could this turn out to be? True love? A mutual romantic companionship? Soulmates? My friends at church told me I was glowing...and I was. Doesn't matter whether it was an illusion, the *feelings* of love were still present. I felt comforted and surprised that my heart was still open to love; that it wasn't totally closed off.

Heroic Heartbeat Lessons

- Now that I know the signs of a future faker, I'll be prepared to recognize if anyone like this shows up again, God forbid. It's not like I'd ask more questions because I asked a boatload of questions, but I realize now that answers will not be truthful or direct. I'd read and listen more carefully between the lines and the signs.
- I learned not to dive so fast into relationships. Take time, spend time, talk to the person and then let them talk and talk and talk. Ask pointed, direct, identifying questions and then trust but verify. If a relationship is supposed to happen, the man will not promise to buy you things or take you places, he will simply do it.
- When you first meet a man, go before God and ask for wisdom and discernment. Ask God to make it clear that if it's not rooted in Him, to break it apart. God is protective of his beloved!

4

NEWLY DIVORCED.
NEWLY SINGLE.

"I learned to not take what people say at face value—trust but verify."

I was newly divorced after a twenty-five-year marriage. The first year of being on my own was the hardest. I had moved from my parents' house straight into marriage as a twenty-year-old and I really didn't know how to be single. I had said yes to Jeff because I wanted to get out from under the control and overprotection of my parents. I had lived under a critical reign of parental rule that undermined the very core of who I was as a person and getting married seemed like a good exit plan. I had been told from childhood that I was only smart enough to be a housewife so I should just find someone who was willing to marry me. That's exactly what I did.

My marriage to Jeff was a rough and rocky road from the beginning—two immature, insecure *kids* trying to fit into each other's lives. I wanted to leave so many times, but I had been taught that you stay with it no matter what, and I was a stay-at-home mom for our two kids, so I felt my options were limited. When Jeff abandoned the marriage after twenty-five tumultuous years, I felt a sense of relief. Doesn't mean my heart wasn't broken and that I didn't experience trauma, but I was glad it was over. I was on my own for the first time in my life… at forty-five.

I settled into the single life. I had fantasized about living a peaceful, calm life since my household had been full of chaos, mostly due to Jeff and the way he harshly disciplined the kids, especially our daughter. Now, I had a new start, a new chance to create a life I had yearned for. After two years, I felt the desire for a relationship. New to the online dating scene, I researched several different websites and settled on two top sites. I carefully crafted my profile, including describing myself as a born-again Christian. Inquiries came in full force, and I was delighted that so many men were showing interest.

But I didn't know what I didn't know.

One day I checked the dating site and a very handsome man named Jalen had reached out with a thoughtful, articulate message. Most of the jokers on the site couldn't complete an intelligible sentence so this man stuck out from the pack. I took the bait. I sent Jalen back a warm message, introducing myself and indicating I'd like to continue the conversation. Jalen and I exchanged several messages on the site until he suggested we speak on the phone. By that time, I was more than willing to talk ear-to-ear with this intelligent dreamboat, so I readily agreed.

He called me, and my first reaction was to melt into a soft ball of putty when I heard his deep, sexy voice. Jalen told me he was very traditional in his views of men, women, and marriage. I told him that June Cleaver was my idol of sorts because of her ability to wear dresses and pearls while she slathered peanut butter on Wally and Beaver's perfectly made sandwiches. Even from that first call, I felt the first twinge of excitement I hadn't felt in a very long time. After talking for several minutes, Jaylen said, "Yes, this is going to work just fine." His comment didn't register. All I knew was that within the month he would be flying from Colorado Springs to visit me in San Diego, California.

When I first spotted Jalen in the airport on a Friday night, my heart leapt with excitement. Walking toward me was a muscular, handsome man with a shaved bald head and a giant smile with beautiful, white teeth glistening as he waved wildly toward me. He carried a full backpack, and it slipped off his shoulder slightly as we eagerly embraced as if we had known each other for years. We couldn't keep our eyes off each other during the drive back to my condominium where I had offered him my couch. When we settled in, he removed two important items from his backpack, and I thought I had died and gone to heaven.

I had previously told Jalen that my Friday night ritual was to eat chips and salsa. When I saw him pull out a bag of tortilla chips and a pint of salsa, I gasped with glee. He then pulled out a DVD about marriage from a popular pastor and we watched it as we feasted on chips and salsa...together. I couldn't wipe the smile off my face. That first weekend with Jalen was sheer heaven... it seemed like we were perfectly matched. Conversation was lively as we got to know each other on a deeper level and shared our views of Christianity, life, marriage, and everything in between. When Jalen left on Sunday, he promised he'd be back soon...and he was.

A month later, Jalen flew into town again on a Friday and the plan was to stay for a week. I welcomed him with an open heart and outstretched arms. The visit began as blissfully as the first one and excitement danced in the atmosphere as Jalen and I expressed our mutual gratitude for having found each other. On Monday morning, I went to work, and Jalen stayed at my place. He had told me during the first visit that he was studying for a specific certification to further himself in his financial/investment job.

No reason to doubt, I knew he'd be studying, and with no car, he couldn't go far. On Wednesday, Jalen called me at work. He said he wanted to buy some sport supplements, but his credit card wasn't working *for some reason* and asked if he could use mine. "Sure," I responded, "no problem." I gave him my only credit card number. A couple of days after that, same scenario. I was at work and Jalen at my place, supposedly studying for his investment certification. He called and said he had someone take his Lexus to the car dealership to get four new tires put on, but his credit card still wasn't working *for some reason*. This time a little more reluctantly, I agreed to the $400+ purchase with Jalen's promise to pay it back. "After all," he said, "He wanted us to be debt-free for our future."

One evening we decided to go to my favorite sushi place. We settled into seats at the counter where we could watch the sushi chefs chopping and dicing and rolling. In the middle of eating sushi, crocodile tears started running down Jalen's face as he pronounced how lucky he felt to have met me. He went on to share how much I meant to him and how he couldn't wait to start our lives together…married. It wasn't a proposal…Jalen had already stated his intentions on his first visit. When it came time to pay, it was no shocker when Jalen's credit card was rendered invalid. I inwardly sighed a bit as I calculated the expenses Jalen had racked up. But, hey, it was all in the name of "we're in this together" mantra.

Later in the week, I wanted to show my new beau off to my co-workers, so we drove to the company where I worked. I was anxious and proud to introduce him to Sandra, Lauren, and Nick. Within a few minutes, Nick had asked Jalen about his time in Tucson, Arizona where Jalen said he had lived for a short time. What Jalen didn't know was that Nick had lived in Tucson for several years. He also asked Jalen about a specific golf course and various places in the surrounding area. After the conversation, I dropped Jalen off at my condo and came back to work. Immediately, Nick confronted me, "He's full of crap." Nick proceeded to explain that Jalen's answers were not accurate and that he was hiding something. I couldn't believe what I was hearing, but I trusted Nick as we had befriended each other as fellow Italians and co-workers. Nick told me to go home and ask Jalen certain questions, which I did.

Instantly Jalen knew he had been busted and his gig was up. He stopped talking to me,; I'm talking total renegade silent treatment. The next day, I took him to the San Diego airport, and as he was getting out of my car, Jalen was promising he'd pay me back every cent. As I drove home, still in disbelief over what was happening, Jalen boldly called and asked me to pay for his flight home as his credit card was still not working. Pretty brazen tactic! Now wise to his antics, I matter-of-factly said, NO!" and hung up. No further word from Jalen except one text that contained a veiled threat, "You'd better watch your back."

I pondered the statement one of my friends had made about the relationship. Suzie had shared a well-worn adage when I told her how wonderful Jalen was, "Ummm, if it sounds too good to be true...and if it looks too good to be true...it probably isn't true." Looking back over the previous few months, the picture became clearer. The set-up, the directed conversations, the lead-up to the credit card use, the promises of a beautiful married life. Why hadn't I seen the signs? Why had I simply taken it all in at face value? I endured the judgement and scolding of friends and family when I revealed I had been swindled and now owed $2,500. I came to refer to Jalen as "the hustler."

I hadn't experienced much of how the world really worked and that there are people with the expressed intent of hurting others and gaining whatever they can for themselves. I later discovered and met three of "the hustler's" ex-wives. Yes, they had married him and soon after divorced. I also learned that his target before me had been an attorney who he swindled out of $18,000 dollars. People tend to think dumb people fall for swindlers, but that's not true. One poll in 2022 revealed that 75% of romance scam targets are college educated and 13% have graduate degrees.

Knowing I had to pay back the money hurt my pocketbook, but my heart hurt mostly from thinking and believing my relationship with Jalen was real when all it was, was an illusion full of lies and deceit. I was thankful I hadn't married him, and I was thankful for Nick who'd spotted the game instantly, which cut the game short.

Heroic Heartbeat Lessons

- I eventually healed from the trauma, the embarrassment, and the credit card payments. I endured comments from family and friends, inferring I was stupid and gullible for falling for an online predator. That hurt…a lot. I stayed close to whomever I could find who was positive and supportive and gracious.

- I learned to not take what people say at face value—trust but verify. That one was the most difficult as I am a very trusting person and believe the best in everyone. It sucks that not everyone has pure motives, but I learned that I must keep my internal radar acutely tuned so I don't fall for every story.
- I learned to Google each new prospective date or love interest to find out all I could about them. Online people finder search engines often offer free trials.
- I learned to ask the *right* questions to draw out inconsistencies in background, employment, and family dynamics. I knew this financial swindler situation would only happen once in my lifetime because now I knew what to look for AND what phrases to listen for and what patterns to recognize.

The bottom line is that I survived. I got smarter, wiser, and savvier.

PART III

LUNATICS

5

THE LONG-TERM NARCISSISTIC HUSBAND

"I struggled for many years, because as a Christian woman, what I was taught and what I knew, I believed I wasn't going be able to divorce this man."

I met Jackson through a long-time friend. They both worked at the same company, and she didn't think of him as a potential someone for me. Initially I wasn't attracted to him, but I was approaching thirty, and although I had become very guarded, there were things about him that I looked at and concluded, "Well, he *is* a Christian, he graduated from a Bible college, he seems to be a responsible man, he owns a home, has a good job, and he›s looking to get remarried and have a family since he and his ex-wife hadn't had any children.

I checked all the boxes and didn't have any reason to say no. He seemed to show characteristics of what I considered to be a leader, and he possessed a strong sense of confidence. I thought, *I might as well give him a try. Nothing else is going on.*

One of the initial red flags was the fact that he was recently divorced, so in my mind, I found myself trying to reconcile, *why would a woman who also called herself a Christian leave a good man, a good Christian man?* I couldn't wrap my head around it, so we had several conversations upfront before we even started dating. His response was to shrug it off, "Well, you know her family of origin and essentially, she was crazy." He portrayed his ex-wife as having all kinds of personal issues with her family and included that she had gone through some counseling, and as a result, left him after six years of marriage.

So that right away was a red flag to me. After we were married, other red flags began to pop up. After we were married, our son Luke was born, and I'd say he was probably two or three years of age when I started taking him to the football games that Jackson officiated. While at one of the games we waved to "daddy" on the sideline as I shouted, "Who's winning?" Jackson looked up at us and threw his arms open and said, "Us...we in the stripes are winning!" I thought, *wow, that's kind of bizarre because games are not typically about the referees.*

Other red flags started to show up. It became a constant cycle of nothing ever getting resolved. I would try to talk to Jackson using the Sandwich Approach; compliment and then say what I was struggling with, and then try to end it on a positive. My "talk" would go in one ear and out the other. I started noticing a pattern. Every Saturday, if he were home, he would moan, "Oh, I'm so tired, I'm so tired, and he would lay on the couch and never do anything with me and the kids." Our life was about *his* activities, *his* work, *his* education, *his* board member work. He was very focused on himself, and I explained it away in my head, *well, he's not satisfied at work, so he's trying to fill that satisfaction in other ways*, and so I would support him thinking I was being a good wife. The truth is that I was constantly being left at home with three small children, being run over by his life and needs. Our life began to crumble.

It was about seven or eight years into our marriage and Luke was about two and a half years old. He was having severe emotional meltdowns and having intense difficulty with everyday tasks in general. I was trying all sorts of discipline plans; everything I could think of with redirection, and reaching out to every resource I could find. Nothing was helping. Jackson wasn't involved whatsoever in the process. In fact, if he did get involved, it would make things worse, and I'd regret even asking him to help. The breaking point was when Luke became so difficult, Jackson told me to send him away, that he was done with him. I glared at him and said, "I will not do that. And if you're telling me to make a choice between you and him, I'm gonna pick him." I continued, "We've got to go to counseling," which to my surprise we did, because it was for Luke. From that point on we were on a downhill slope but through counseling things began to become much clearer to me. We went to counseling for a year and a half, and as the counselor wisely discerned, it was no longer about Luke. The counselor knew there were much deeper issues at play.

Jackson and I were married just shy of twenty years if you count the legal separation. Our divorce was final in 2021 so really it was twenty-two years because a two-and-a-half-year court battle ensued before the divorce was finalized.

Looking back in retrospect, narcissistic abuse circumstances became a way of life. I had our daughters in rapid succession, so we'd had three children in four years. I later found out through testing that Luke was on the spectrum when he was diagnosed with a non-verbal learning disability called Asperger's. It became clear why he had such difficulty with everyday life. Jackson did whatever he wanted to do, so I was home a lot alone with the children and not having family or anyone to help. I had supportive friends, and I was thankful for that.

If Jackson wanted to have sex and I said I felt sick or I wasn't feeling well, he would often wake me up in the middle of the night to get what he wanted because life was all about him getting whatever he wanted when he wanted. Sometimes I would say no in what I thought was a non-threatening way, "I just don't feel well" trying not to make it personal against him, and he would immediately react with a physical rejection of pushing me away. He'd push me back over and then would not speak to me. No understanding, no empathy, no compassion. It was a consistent pattern.

Another instance had to do with our home computer. I homeschooled our children, and the computer we were using was old, it hardly ever worked, and it caused intense frustration on my part because I couldn't efficiently bring up the kid's school assignments and other resources we needed. This went on for probably two or three years, and when I explained to Jackson about it, he would say, "Well, that's just a user error, you don't know how to use it." He had a high-tech, new computer for work and exhibited a total lack of empathy and caring for what I went through with our crappy home computer day after day. I was cautious about our finances and didn't want to put us in a bad financial situation by buying a new home computer, but anyone who has homeschooled knows how crucial it is to have access to a decent computer. As the head of our household, Jackson consistently demonstrated no sense of, "Let me help," or "Let me figure out a way to relieve you of this frustration you're having."

Jackson's verbal attacks greatly intensified and ramped up when through continued counseling I started to learn about and create boundaries for myself. His attacks came in the form of continual blaming and gaslighting. If I attempted to help him understand some of the things he struggled with because of his childhood, things he needed healing from, it just got turned around on me. He'd retort, "Well, look at you! You have a problem with men because of your mom and the way you were raised."

When things really intensified, he'd ramp it up even more with personal verbal assaults like, "You're looking old." Likewise, when I decided that I needed to start doing something with my life after the kids were older, I pursued going back to graduate school and he would tell me, "You're not that smart." He never owned responsibility for anything, nor did he attempt to get our family help or get me help with the kids. Luke's Asperger's continued to get worse and worse. Occasionally, I would suggest to him that he learn some parenting skills because he would shame the kids or be ultra harsh in his discipline. I would tell him, "That's not helpful, can we find a better way?" His response? "No! Parenting is common sense; I don't need to learn that." Our life consisted of him saying, "I'm tired, I'm going to go back to school and get my Master's," never thinking about how any of it would affect the kids and me. Whatever he wanted to do, he did.

I struggled for many years because as a Christian woman, what I was taught and what I knew, I believed I wasn't going be able to divorce this man. I kept telling myself, driving myself, even forcing myself to find ways to "love" him, yet it only drove me to dislike him more and even hate him. It was getting to the point where I began to resent God for making me stay married to him. The first counselor introduced a word that resonated within the core of my being when he asked, "Are you familiar with the term narcissism?" That was the beginning of the end for me.

I tried to figure out how to stay well while staying married, and I took a deeper dive into counseling. All I knew was that life wasn't working the way I was trying to work with Jackson. I mused *how can I learn to stay well with this man? Because we have these kids and all I have to do is get them graduated and then I can try to figure out a way to live my own life.* I also took a deeper dive into God's word and dug into more education around what was really going on. Through digging through layers and unveiling the truth through continual counseling, I began to better understand Jackson as a narcissist and all the ways in which that manifested in our marriage and family life. What I came to understand was that the success rate of a narcissist fully recovering is next to impossible, and I also didn't realize that what had been happening to me was abuse.

It was hard for me to even say the word "abuse" word because he wasn't physically abusing me, he wasn't having affairs, he wasn't drinking, he wasn't addicted, he wasn't doing drugs. I think in his mind he was checking all the boxes and that he was a good husband. In the meantime, me and the kids were falling apart. We were dying spiritually, emotionally, mentally. One of my daughters, Laurie, was having a lot of headaches and my other daughter Cassandra was displaying physical ticks as a manifestation of her stress and anxiety. Luke continued to experience worsening meltdowns, and by this time he was getting physical with me which resulted in having to place him in three mental hospitals. In the meantime, I continued with counseling and education on narcissists.

I recognized that the situation wasn't going to change; I also started recognizing that it was abuse, and Jackson had made it clear that he refused to make any changes. He would go to counseling for a short time and would end up saying, I'm good, I'm done. I met with the last counselor Jackson went to and I gained intense clarity that nothing was going to change, and that I needed to start to move on and plan my exit for the health and well-being of me and my kids.

As I had previously felt that divorce hadn't been an option for me, I had now had gained real clarity around the truth of scripture. I went back to school and got my graduate degree, and I secured a job. I recognized that a divorce would be very contentious, and I tried to figure out the right timing to make it happen. The final breaking point was when I sent Luke to a boys therapeutic home to get help for him. After he was finished with the therapeutic program, I sent him off to college.

I made it clear that my son was not to return home for long periods because it would be like an alcoholic going back to a bar and expecting not to drink. Things with the family weren't changing because Jackson wasn't changing. However, I was changing and becoming a healthier person and holding to my boundaries. He convinced me that Luke should come back home during school breaks and summers but being around his father triggered Luke to go back to his old ways. He started to be abusive again. That was the tipping point to show me I had to leave. I had told my girls, "We aren't going to live like this anymore." I had saved up enough money to file for a divorce and start to make our exit.

Heroic Heartbeat Lessons

- I would say do your own personal work. Evaluate yourself and your family system before you think about getting into a relationship. Make yourself as emotionally, spiritually, mentally, and physically healthy as you can be because anybody coming out of a family must learn what their childhood family dynamics were, identifying the unhealthy and healthy parts, and how they fit into the family structure. Get yourself to a place where you understand yourself, what you believe in, your values, and learn to set healthy boundaries that work for you. I think a lot of women don't understand that boundaries are good, boundaries are healthy, but you must know what your boundaries are.
- I learned that when you marry a narcissist it is often typical that you grew up with a narcissist. I was very comfortable being with someone who was emotionally unavailable because that's what I experienced as a child. Once I understood my family dynamics, I understood why I chose a person who was unhealthy. It was because I was unhealthy. I realize now that I was only able to pick

someone who was as healthy as I was. As I look back even now, I ask, *Why did I feel so comfortable with him?* It was because I felt uncomfortable with men who paid attention to me, who listened to me, who took interest in me.

- Do your work in studying the scripture because scripture interprets scripture. I learned so much about how many in the church use scriptures that are taken out of context to keep women in bondage. This is how Satan works. He will use God's word and twist it just enough to keep you in bondage.

- The biggest takeaway for me was not taking what someone says at face value. I'm going to take a deeper dive and see God's character and what God is trying to say in the specific passage. What was Paul trying to say? What was Moses trying to say? What was the reasoning behind what they were saying?" Because when you take a deeper dive, it is never God's character for women to stay in any type of abusive situation in the name of an institution called marriage. Nor does the saying, "it's your cross to bear" or "God will get the glory for your suffering." It's all lies. God gets no glory nor is He pleased when women enable abusive men to treat them with such treachery. God does care about marriage, but not above the people in it.

6

NARCISSISTIC ABUSE ON STEROIDS

"As of this writing, I have emotionally detoxed and am discovering new strengths within myself every single day."

I met Cassius through a roommate. I took him to the house where my roommate and I lived, and in all honesty, I have no idea what attracted me to him in the first place because when I think back, he wasn't an attractive person. All I know is during that time of my life I was emotionally bankrupt, and I needed somebody to be there, and he just happened to be there, but not in a good way. After that, I couldn't get rid of him.

It was only a couple of weeks into our relationship when the first red flag, or I should say, blaring siren, surfaced. We woke up one morning and I decided I was going to make pancakes. I don't cook, so making pancakes is kind of a big deal. Happy with the results, I took them into the bedroom so we could eat them, and I remember Cassius being a total jerk, saying "I don't want them anymore, leave me alone," as he rolled over and went back to sleep. I had taken the time to make breakfast, and yet, here I was, sitting, waiting for him to wake up, which wasn't until hours later. I had saved some pancakes for him, but he threw them in the trash and made his own.

Another gigantic red flag was that Cassius would hack into my Facebook account and register me for dating websites, which later meant that he would yell at me, accusing me of signing up for them. He wouldn't listen to my defense. It was a losing battle, but I continued to stay with him.

Over time, and many other instances, I don't know if *he* got worse, or *I* got worse with dealing with it—it's hard to tell. What I do know is that after some time his treatment completely wore me down. His MO was to break me down so he could come in and save me, when, really, I would never have broken down in the first place had it not been for him. This happened over and over and over for close to a decade. He would break me down to the point where I was suicidal and then he would say, "Hey, baby, let me come and rescue you!" I'd find a note from him in my journal telling me how much he admired me, what a strong person he thought I was, and how much he cared about me. At the time, it was enough, because I wanted his approval. I wanted him to love me, and I valued his opinion of me. So, finding those notes made me think, *oh, well, he does care*. By this time, we had had a baby together so now he and I were linked for life.

The final straw came when I realized I couldn't function normally on a daily basis. I was super depressed most of the time and many days I couldn't even get out of bed to take care of my child because of how miserable and oppressed I felt. At one point, I tried to go to school, and despite completing the paperwork to enroll, because of the demeaning things Cassius was telling me and how he made me feel, I didn't believe I was equal to anyone else in the school. I attended one semester at The Art Institute but found that I couldn't function. I couldn't look people in the eye due to how I felt about myself. I didn't think I was good enough to be there with the other students because I felt so less than. I dropped out. That was my tipping point to get away.

I had wanted to escape for a long time before that but I couldn't because I didn't have anywhere else to go. My thoughts churned within me *I can't leave and take my child, because if I leave, my daughter and I will have to go out on the street because I don't have anywhere else to go. If I leave, I'll have to leave my child and I can't leave my child with him.* A massive internal battle raged within my mind and heart; *I can't take this anymore. I have to go. I don't care what I have to do. I don't care where I have to go. I just have to go before I succumb to what I believe his goal in life is: to make me kill myself.* It disgusts me now to know the mental power that someone else can have over another person.

I repeated the cycle of leaving and coming back to him for ten years. To this day he's my emergency contact. He's the one I call if I go to jail, the one I call if I go to the hospital. I still go back to him in a way, but he doesn't have the same control over me that he once did. I was able to break the power of his attempts at making me feel horrible about myself. You might not believe this but the way I was able to find myself again was through going to jail. Because every time I would go to jail I was away from his influence, and I could be myself. It was in jail that I was able to regain my own self-awareness, or whatever you want to call it.

I had left Cassius a few times for other men but always ended up coming back. I finally let go of his control over me when I left him for ME, not for anybody else. When I left for good, I was homeless on the streets, or I stayed in a nature reserve that I called "the jungle," alone. I know for certain that was when I was able to finally release some of his hold over me. And oddly enough, that's when we started to become *somewhat* friends. The tie is always going to be there to a certain extent. We have a child together. But we're disconnected in that he won't ever be able to put me in that place of despair and destruction.

He still tries to loop me in, and the whole reason he kept our daughter when I was homeless was because it was the only way he had to control me. It's not like he wanted to spend time with her. He never did any activities with her; he would drop her off and leave. I can easily say that he never really wanted her, although I think in his own very flawed way that he loves her. But he kept her in his house mostly because that was the only way he could control me.

As of this writing, I have emotionally detoxed and am discovering new strengths within myself every single day. I moved to a tropical location and the beauty of this place overwhelms me. I'm involved in my start-up business, and I have my daughter with me now.

I talk to women who have gone through remarkably similar situations as I did, and they all say the same thing: you feel so alone when you're going through it. Having already walked through it, I'm able to show other girls that they're not alone, that I get where they're at, that I understand the levels of despair and hurt, and the emotional and mental damage that can be inflicted on them by another person. I want to shout from the rooftop that if you're going through a narcissistic abuse situation, you're not alone! It's crucial to find a community that fits who you are because when you're going through narcissistic abuse, the thing you want to do is isolate, yet that's when you need your tribe the most. I believe there is a reason I had to go through those deep waters as I don't think I would be the person I am today without having gone through all of that. I'm happy with who I am today, and I know who I am today, and that's why community is so important.

Heroic Heartbeat Lessons

- A lot of what a narcissist does, what Cassius did, is that they try to make you doubt your own reality. They try to tell you that things didn't happen the way they happened. They'll tell you, "no, it happened this way" and they make you the bad guy in all the stories. Eventually, if you don't have someone to fact check with, you'll start to believe it. You must have at least one trusted friend who you can call and ask, "Is this really how the circumstance happened because this is what I think happened. This is what he's telling me and I'm starting to think it's true." Your friend who was also there can tell you, "No, that's not how it went down." I've found that with narcissists, the whole intent of gaslighting is to make you doubt your own reality.

- Another important thing to do is to set strong boundaries. If you choose to stay in a narcissistic relationship, or you can't sever ties because you have a child together, develop some ground rules that work for you. You can propose communicating solely via text or email, which will allow you more time to think about your responses (not reactions) and it will also document all communication.

- Avoid emotional entanglements. Your child's other parent may take pleasure in witnessing your anxiety or distress, so don't give them that satisfaction. When dealing with conflicts, refrain from involving your child as a messenger, mediator,

or information gatherer. Keep communication directly between you and your ex to maintain a clear and healthy approach.
- Take advantage of court services. Guardian ad litem (GAL) is a court-appointed (neutral) person who looks out for the "best interests of a child." You can request that one be appointed.
- Ultimately, what I discovered is that Cassius is just a big bully. I don't know why he picked me to take all his bullying out on, because I met a couple of his ex-girlfriends and they both told me, "Jocelyn, he was never like that with me." I don't know why it was me; maybe I was vulnerable at the time I met him. Most of the things he threatened me with that I had been so afraid of were only threats. I found out that he wasn't really going to follow through with most of them. He delivered his threats with the intent to make me conform to what he wanted me to do, and it worked for a long time.
- Some signs to watch out for are if the person is trying to tell you that what you remember is not what really happened, then that's a bully. If they're trying to isolate you and they're able to make you completely ignore all your friends, that's a bully.
- If you're giving up what you love to do for what they love, then something's wrong. And, if they make you feel like it's not like that, there's something wrong.
- Another takeaway from having lived through the experience is knowing who I am and being happy

with who I am and where I am today. It's not like before I met him, I was happy. I was miserable then, too, but I was happier. It's significant to be able to be genuinely happy with who you are and to be okay with living life alone on your terms.

- Watch out for relationship patterns. Even now, I find myself dating guys who try to put me in the same predicament as Cassius or elicit feelings of giving up what I love for them. But now I'm able to spot it and remove myself from the situation easier and much quicker. You may be screaming to yourself: *this will never happen to me again!* I'm here to tell you to give yourself some grace; I'm still struggling with it; every day is a battle. But what I do know is that I'll never let somebody take me to the places that Cassius took me, mentally and emotionally. Walk in your internal strength and walk in your worth.

CONCLUSION

*A*s I close out this book, my heart is filled with a mix of sorrow and determination. There are so many untold stories that could have found a place within these pages. The landscape of my personal sphere of contacts is littered with broken hearts and shattered dreams. Each shattered dream and broken heart serve as a stark reminder of the pain endured in the pursuit of love and acceptance—*the love of potential*. We believed in the one who turned out to be anything but what we hoped. After all…

We thought *he* was the one.

We thought *he* truly saw our value.

We thought *he* would fulfill our longing to be wholeheartedly and wholly loved for who we are.

The *love of potential* keeps us tethered to seeking validation from outside forces without realizing our intrinsic worth. Romance scammers, future fakers, and narcissistic abusers can *smell* a lack of self-confidence and vulnerability from a mile away. The qualities we possess—a nurturing, kind, caring, compassionate, authentic, giving spirit—are the very traits absent in their lives. Their presence preys on our vulnerabilities, exploiting our caring and compassionate spirits for their selfish gains. Typically, the romance scammer or narcissistic abuser's personality type is steeped in shame and insecurity and the only way they can stay in control and dominance is to verbally chop down their targets; to attempt to wipe away the wonderful traits that remind them of who *they* really are...lonely, unsatisfied, unhappy, and unfulfilled.

But amid the darkness lies a glimmer of hope—a realization that we are worth more than the validation we seek from those who cannot reciprocate our love. The recognition of our own intrinsic worth is the key to breaking free from the clutches of romance scammers, future fakers, and narcissistic abusers.

The women who relived their stories by contributing to this book poured their wounded, yet now wonderfully whole souls, onto these pages. I trust that by reading this book you have found a guiding light that shines forth insight and awareness. Beyond just a cautionary tale, I yearn for this book to be a beacon of hope, illuminating the path to a life free from inauthentic relationships and situationships.

As I stated in the Introduction, I deliberately refrained from using the term "victim" because we are not defined by the actions of those who hurt us. We have the power to choose how we respond to adversity. We are survivors, but more than that, we are thrivers! It takes immense courage to heal from the wounds of a destructive relationship. However, once we do the work to heal and overcome a destructive relationship, once we forgive the perpetrator and forgive ourselves, we can thrive more than we ever have in our lives and businesses.

I know transformation is possible because I've lived it! Reclaiming my heart continues to come through the power of my personal relationship with Christ. He reminds me in His Word of who I am IN HIM, His immense love and care for me, and the names He calls me by (Hephzibah, meaning *my delight is in her*, His workmanship, His beloved, the apple of His eye).

Within the hedges of healing and forgiveness lies the potential for newfound strength—a strength that allows us to thrive beyond our wildest dreams. Despite the pain, we can rise above, learning to love ourselves wholly and unconditionally.

May this book serve as a testament to the resilience of a woman's spirit, a testament to the fact that we can reclaim our lives and rebuild ourselves from the ground up. May this book be a source of inspiration for those seeking a brighter, more authentic future—a future where love, respect, and genuine connections flourish. May this book serve as a reminder that we are deserving of every ounce of love, positivity, affirmation, and happiness this world has to offer, and with determination, we can embrace life in all its fullness and richness.

Now go forth, embrace the strength within you, and fiercely live your best, most empowered life—refusing to compromise who you are for anyone!

10 RED FLAGS YOU ABSOLUTELY, POSITIVELY MUST WATCH OUT FOR

1. **Love Bombing** – How strong is the person coming on? Do you feel as if you've been transported to paradise by the way they treat you? Are they going overboard with compliments and gifts? If someone who hardly knows you is showering you obsessively with gifts and attention, it's a red flag. True love takes time to develop; it's not a microwave proposition.

2. **Promises, Promises** – Is he promising exotic, lavish vacations and trips, perfume, jewelry, and other gifts…all in the future? He may say, "It's going to be a surprise." If the promises come to nothing, it's a red flag. A *real* man's actions will line up with his words and he'll simply do those things, he won't promise them.

3. **Limited Availability** – Does he give you free reign to call him any day or evening of the week, taking into account work activities? If there are certain days/

nights he cannot be reached and comes up with a lame excuse for why he isn't available, this is a red flag. A man who's sincerely interested in you will demonstrate full transparency with his schedule.

4. **Degrades then rescues** – This is a favorite tool of the narcissistic abuser. They break you down verbal chop by verbal chop, and when they see your shoulders droop and a defeated look in your eyes, they'll ease up. They might even do something nice for you or throw you a verbal bone…until you do something else to annoy them. Be on the lookout for this destructive cycle because it's a red flag. The power of life and death is in the tongue and a *real* man will uplift and speak life into you.

5. **Vague answers** when you ask about his life – Does he talk in circles, often contradicting himself? Red flag. Have you caught him in lies? Red flag. It's imperative that you listen very carefully to their facts and timelines. Don't be afraid to ask clarifying questions, but be aware that you're probably not going to get straight answers.

6. **Story concoctions about his credit card** – Has he told you stories about how he had to get a new credit card and for some reason it isn't working? Has he asked you if you'll charge something one time because he's located at a faraway military base or he's an offshore oil rig worker and doesn't have access to his money? Major red flag. Make sure the puzzle pieces fit!

7. **Your gut tells you something doesn't feel right** – Women's intuition is your best friend! If something inside you is telling you that something is amiss, pay attention to that because it's an internal red flag.

8. **The no-meet friends' zone** – He's not interested in meeting your friends and he doesn't want you to meet his friends. This is because he doesn't intend to stick around, or he knows his friends are wise to his tactics. Another oft-used tactic is to divide and conquer; his attempts to alienate you from your friends and family. Not wanting to cross social circles or if he creates animosity within your own circle is a red flag.

9. **Asking about YOU** – Does he ask you about your work, what you do? Note: *he should never ask about your salary!* If he does, run like the dickens!! Does he show interest in your profession, your hobbies? If he only focuses on his endeavors, his schedule, his work, it's a red flag. A *real* man shows his care for you through genuine, authentic, direct compliments directed at YOU as a person.

10. **Saying I love you waaay too soon** – Has he professed his love for you after three dates, or after only a month of seeing each other? Red flag alert. He doesn't love you—he doesn't even know you! Love grows over time. When you plant flower seeds, the flowers don't bloom a week later. It takes time to develop love.

ABOUT THE AUTHOR

*M*ichelle Hill is a Book and Publishing Consultant and Founder of Winning Proof, a company helping sports and business professionals get their books written, published, and promoted. Her impressive roster of clientele includes pro athletes, sports agents, coaches, NFL GMs, high-level performance trainers, sport psychologists, leadership coaches, and auto dealership owners and GMs.

She is an ongoing moderator for the annual Carolina Book and Writer Conference and host of the YouTube podcast, *Winning Proof Unscripted* where she engages in captivating conversations with fascinating guests.

She is the author of 4 books: *Bathroom Prayers—Inspiring Thoughts While You're on the Pot* under the pen name Anita Flushing, *From Pen to Published—A Blueprint for Success* which she co-authored with former NFL player, Brandon Williams, and two bestselling, multiple award-winning children's books she co-authored with her cousin, Joy VanDertuin, *Gizelle's Silly, Soggy Day* and *Gizelle's Whimsical Wintery Day*.

By writing *The Heart Swindler*, Michelle's mission is to walk with women through the heartbreaking aftershock of surviving romance scammers and narcissistic abusers. There's much work to be done and Michelle's goal is to journey alongside women, helping them to become the best, most confident version of themselves.

Looking for private, personal support as you navigate forward from relationship deception to find healing and wholeness?

Heart Restoration Conversation

During your 45-minute session, Michelle will listen to your story with an empathic ear <u>and no judgment</u> as you pour out your heartache after relationship deception. Michelle knows what it feels like, and she can offer guidance and specialized resources to help you reclaim your heart and find your way back to wholeness.

Healing begins here!

Book your Heart Restoration Session today at

https://calendly.com/winningproof/heart-restoration-session

Afterward, we can decide if the next right step is to work together further through Gentle Guidance Sessions.

Through ongoing Gentle Guidance Sessions, I'll guide you toward:

- Finding lasting forgiveness
- Making peace with yourself
- Reclaiming your fractured heart
- Building confidence for your future dating decisions
- Accessing meaningful resources that help you move ahead

Special Bonus Gifts from Michelle

Being a survivor of a liar, loser, or lunatic from relationship deception leaves most women feeling betrayed, wounded, and left to deal with a lot of heartache.

I've personally experienced this heartbreak, and I know all too well how challenging it is to find support and resources to heal and work toward rebuilding your life and reclaiming your heart.

This is why I created TWO VALUABLE BONUS GIFTS to help you heal as you move forward on your journey toward wholeness.

Get your bonuses at:
https://heartswindler.com/Book-Bonuses

Bonus #1 – Resources to Inform and Heal

Michelle's thoughtfully curated collection of resources is designed to support, educate, and inspire you on your journey toward healing and transformation.

Bonus #2 - Heartbeats to Healing: 8 Self-Care Ways to Heal from Relationship Deception

An inspiring guide to help you regain your confidence, self-worth, and inner contentment after experiencing relationship betrayal.

CONNECT WITH MICHELLE

*A*s you've learned from reading this book, Michelle is on a mission to guide and empower women, helping them heal and flourish after romantic deception.

Michelle says, "Let's link arms as we reclaim strength, renew trust, and embrace love in the wake of heartache."

She'd love to share with your women's group or serve as a speaker at your upcoming conference, retreat, meeting or on your podcast.

Please email her at michelle@heartswindler.com.

Let's connect on social media:

Facebook: www.facebook.com/winningproof

LinkedIn: www.linkedin.com/in/winningproof

If you're a fan of this book, please tell others...

- Write about *The Heart Swindler* on your blog and social media channels.
- Feature Michelle on your podcast or radio/TV broadcast.
- Suggest this book to your friends, family, neighbors, and coworkers.
- Write an authentic, positive review on Amazon.com.
- Take a selfie of you holding the book, post, and tag me on your social media channels.
- Purchase additional copies for the women in your life or to give away as gifts.

Personal Reflection

Personal Reflection

Personal Reflection

Personal Reflection

www.ingramcontent.com/pod-product-compliance
Lightning Source LLC
Chambersburg PA
CBHW072213070526
44585CB00015B/1325